Liverpool

Quiz Book

101 Questions That Will Test Your Knowledge Of This Prestigious Club

By Chris Carpenter

Published by Glowworm Press

Liverpool Football Club

This book contains one hundred and one informative and entertaining trivia questions with multiple choice answers. You will find some easy, and some more challenging and this entertaining informative book will test your knowledge and memory of the club's long and successful history. You will be asked a wide range of topics associated with Liverpool Football Club for you to test yourself. You will be asked about players, managers, legends, transfer deals, opponents, fixtures, trophies, honours and terrace songs amongst other things thereby guaranteeing you both hours of fun and an educational experience. This Liverpool Quiz Book is enjoyable, informative and fun and will offer entertainment for Liverpool FC followers regardless of age; as well as testing your understanding of **Liverpool Football Club**.

Disclaimer

Let's start with some relatively easy questions.

1. When were Liverpool founded?
   A. 1890
   B. 1892
   C. 1894

2. What is Liverpool's nickname?
   A. The Red Devils
   B. The Red Robins
   C. The Reds

3. Where does Liverpool play their home games?
   A. Anfield
   B. Goodison Park
   C. Melwood

4. What is the stadium's capacity?
   A. 50,407
   B. 54,074
   C. 57,470

5. Who or what is the club mascot?
   A. Mighty Red
   B. Brian Bird
   C. Ryan Red Nose

6. Who has made the most appearances for the club in total?
   A. Ian Callaghan
   B. Emlyn Hughes
   C. Billy Liddell

7. Who is the club's record goal scorer?
   A. Robbie Fowler
   B. Roger Hunt
   C. Ian Rush

8. Who is the fastest ever goal scorer for the club?
   A. Jack Balmer
   B. Robbie Fowler
   C. Daniel Sturridge

9. What song do the players run out to?
   A. Theme Tune to Z Cars
   B. Go Go Liverpool Go
   C. You Will Never Walk Alone

10. Which of these is a well known pub near the ground?
    A. The Albert
    B. The Victoria
    C. Albert and Victoria

OK, so here are the answers to the first ten questions. If you get eight or more right, you are doing very well so far, but don't get too cocky, as the questions do get harder.

A1. Liverpool were founded in 1892.

A2. Liverpool's official nickname is The Reds.

A3. Liverpool plays their home games at Anfield which has been their home since their formation in 1892. Not many people know but it was originally the home of Everton between 1884 to 1891 before they moved to Goodison Park.

A4. The current stadium has a seating capacity of 54,074, with plans to expand this in the next few years.

A5. Mighty Red is the controversial mascot who was unveiled in 2012. He is a five feet tall excitable young Liver Bird - a Liver Bird that has teeth and a beak. He has divided opinion amongst many Liverpool fans who question why the club needs such a mascot at all.

A6. Ian Callaghan made a total of 857 appearances for the club. Legend.

A7. Ian Rush scored a grand total of 346 goals for the club, 229 in the league. Roger Hunt scored 245 goals in the league, and 286 in total to be the second highest goal scorer.

A8. Back in February 1938, Jack Balmer scored just ten seconds after kick off in a 3-1 victory over Everton at Goodison.

A9. The players run out to You Will Never Walk Alone.

A10. Arguably the most well popular and well known pub near the ground is The Albert, right next to the Kop. Be prepared to queue for a pint though!

OK, back to the questions.

11. What is the highest number of goals that Liverpool has scored in a league season?
    A. 101
    B. 102
    C. 106

12. What is the fewest number of goals that Liverpool has conceded in a league season?
    A. 16 in 42 games (1978-79, First Division)
    B. 17 in 42 games (1953-54, First Division)
    C. 18 in 42 games (1961-62, First Division)

13. Who has scored the most penalties for the club?
    A. Ian Callaghan
    B. Steven Gerrard
    C. Roger Hunt

14. Who has made the most league appearances for the club?
    A. Ian St John
    B. Ian Callaghan
    C. Roger Hunt

15. What is the home end of the ground known as?
    A. The Chop
    B. The Kop
    C. The Slop

16. What is the club's record attendance?
    A. 60,059
    B. 61,905
    C. 63,590

17. Where is Liverpool's training ground?
    A. Finch Farm
    B. Melwood
    C. Carrington Heath

18. What is the name of the road the ground is on?
    A. Kemlyn Road
    B. Dinorwic Road
    C. Anfield Road

19. Which stand has the biggest capacity?
    A. Main Stand
    B. The Kop
    C. Centenary Stand

20. What is the size of the pitch?
    A. 110 x 75 yards
    B. 100 x 72 yards
    C. 110 x 70 yards

Here are the answers to this block of questions.

A11. The highest number of league goals scored was 106 in the 1895-96 season in the old Second Division. Recently, a staggering 101 goals were scored in the 2013-14 season in the Premier League.

A12. The fewest number of goals conceded in a season was 16 in 42 games in the old First Division, back in 1978-79.

A13. The player who has scored the most penalties for the club is Steve Gerrard. He scored 46 out of the 53 penalties he took for the club.

A14. Toxteth born local lad Ian Callaghan made the most league appearances for the club, 640 in total, covering the years 1960-1978.

A15. The home end of the ground is known as the Kop which got its name from the Boer wars in South Africa. In 1906 Liverpool Echo sports editor Ernest Edwards christened it the Spion Kop; it was so named as the original open air embankment resembled a hill near Ladysmith, South Africa, that was the scene of the Battle of Spion Kop in January 1900 during the Second Boer War.

A16. The record attendance is 61,905 for a match against Wolverhampton Wanderers on 2nd February 1952.

A17. Melwood is the training ground, located in the West Derby area of the city. It is separate from the Liverpool Academy, which is based in Kirkby.

A18. Anfield Stadium is on Anfield Road. Anfield is a residential district of Liverpool full of late 19th century terraced houses. Anfield derives from the old English 'Hanging Field' which means deeply sloping (hanging) fields, from when the area was grazing land back in the early 1800s.

A19. The newly extended Main Stand has the largest capacity in the ground with room for 20,500, all seated of course. The new dugout sports bar within the stand is well worth a visit if you get the chance.

A20. The size of the pitch at the ground is 110 yards long x 75 yards wide, which is exactly the same as Stamford Bridge, the home of Chelsea FC. By way of comparison, Wembley's pitch is 115 yards long by 75 yards wide.

Now we move onto some questions about the club's records.

21. What is the club's record win in any competition?
    A. 11-0
    B. 11-1
    C. 11-2

22. Who did they beat?
    A. Sandvikens
    B. Stockholm
    C. Strømsgodset

23. In which season?
    A. 1971-1972
    B. 1972-1973
    C. 1973-1974

24. What is the club's record win in the league?
    A. 9-1
    B. 10-1
    C. 11-1

25. Who did they beat?
    A. Rochdale
    B. Rotherham Town
    C. Wrexham

26. Who is the club's honorary life president?
    A. David Coleman
    B. David Dimbleby
    C. David Moores

27. What is the club's record defeat?
    A. 1-7
    B. 1-8
    C. 1-9

28. Who against?
    A.   Birmingham City
    B.   Arsenal
    C.   Sunderland

29. Which Liverpool band recorded You Will
    Never Walk Alone?
    A.   The Beatles
    B.   Gerry and the Pacemakers
    C.   The Hideaways

30. Who has scored the most hat tricks for
    Liverpool?
    A.   Robbie Fowler
    B.   Gordon Hodgson
    C.   Roger Hunt

Here are the answers to this block of questions.

A21. Liverpool's record win is 11-0.

A22. They beat Swedish side Strømsgodset 11-0 in the UEFA Cup Winners' Cup.

A23. The date for Liverpool's record win was on the 17th September 1974, hence the 1975-75 season.

A24. Liverpool's record league win is 10-1.

A25. Rotherham Town were thrashed 10-1 in Liverpool's record league win way back on the 18th February 1896.

A26. The club's honorary life president is David Moores.

A27. Liverpool's record defeat is 1-9.

A28. Liverpool's record defeat was by Birmingham City in the old Second Division on the 11th December 1954.

A29. You Will Never Walk Alone is a tune from the 1945 musical Carousel. The song has been recorded by many artists including Frank Sinatra, Elvis Presley and Andy Williams but the Liverpool connection is with Gerry and The Pacemakers who recorded it in 1963; and it is their rendition that is played at Anfield. In 1965 Bill Shankly picked this song as his final selection for Desert Island Discs.

A30. Gordon Hodgson scored an incredible 17 hat tricks for the club between 1926 and 1935. Ian Rush scored 16 hat tricks in total between 1980 and 1996, and Robbie Fowler scored 10 hat tricks in total, including 8 hat tricks in the Premier League - a record for the Premier League.

Now we move onto questions about the club's trophies.

31. When did the club win their first League title?
    A. 1900
    B. 1911
    C. 1921

32. When did the club win their first FA Cup?
    A. 1955
    B. 1965
    C. 1975

33. How many times has Liverpool won the League?
    A. 16
    B. 17
    C. 18

34. How many times have Liverpool won the FA Cup?
    A. 6
    B. 7
    C. 8

35. How many times have Liverpool won the League Cup?
    A. 7
    B. 8
    C. 9

36. How many times have Liverpool won the European Cup / Champions League?
    A. 3
    B. 4
    C. 5

37. Who was the last captain to lift the League trophy?
    A. Steven Gerrard

B. Alan Hansen
C. Graeme Souness

38. Who was the last captain to lift the FA Cup?
    A. Ian Callaghan
    B. Steven Gerrard
    C. Emlyn Hughes

39. Who was the last captain to lift the League
    Cup?
    A. Kenny Dalglish
    B. Steven Gerrard
    C. Graeme Souness

40. Who was the last captain to lift the Champions
    League Trophy?
    A. Steven Gerrard
    B. Sami Hyypia
    C. Graeme Souness

Here are the answers to this block of questions.

A31. The club won their first league title in 1901

A32. The club won their first FA Cup on the 1st May 1965, beating Leeds United 2-1 after extra time in the final, with the goals scored by Roger Hunt and Ian St John.

A33. The club have won a grand total of 18 league titles.

A34. In total, Liverpool has won the FA Cup 7 times, with the most recent being in 2006.

A35. In total, Liverpool has won the League Cup 8 times, an English record.

A36. In Istanbul, we won it five times.

A37. Alan Hansen was the last Liverpool captain to lift the League title, back in 1989-90.

A38. In May 2006 at the Millennium Stadium in Cardiff, Steven Gerrard scored a last minute equaliser against West Ham, and Liverpool eventually won the trophy after a penalty shoot out, with captain and man of the match Gerrard lifting the trophy.

A39. In February 2012 at the Millennium Stadium in Cardiff, Liverpool eventually won the trophy after a penalty shoot out against Cardiff City, with captain Steven Gerrard lifting the trophy.

A40. Who can ever forget the 25th May 2005, and Istanbul, when Stevie G lifted the trophy after one of the most dramatic fight backs in European history, after Liverpool came from 0-3 down at half time, to draw the game 3-3 and eventually win the trophy in a penalty shoot-out.

I hope you're having fun, and getting most of the answers right.

41. What is the record transfer fee paid?
    - A. £55 million
    - B. £65 million
    - C. £75 million

42. Who was the record transfer fee paid for?
    - A. Naby Keita
    - B. Sadio Mane
    - C. Virgil van Dijk

43. What is the record transfer fee received?
    - A. £75 million
    - B. £112 million
    - C. £142 million

44. Who was the record transfer fee received for?
    - A. Luis Suarez
    - B. Fernando Torres
    - C. Philippe Coutinho

45. Who was the first Liverpool player to play for England?
    - A. Frank Becton
    - B. Ron Yeats
    - C. Ian Callaghan

46. Who has won the most international caps whilst a Liverpool player?
    - A. Steven Gerrard
    - B. Robbie Fowler
    - C. Fernando Torres

47. Who has scored the most international goals whilst a Liverpool player?
    - A. Michael Owen
    - B. Steven Gerrard

C. Ian Rush

48. Who is the youngest player ever to represent the club?
    A. Jerome Sinclair
    B. Michael Owen
    C. Raheem Sterling

49. Who is the youngest ever goal scorer for Liverpool?
    A. Michael Owen
    B. Jordan Rossiter
    C. Raheem Sterling

50. What position did the club finish at the end of the 2017/18 season?
    A. 2nd
    B. 3rd
    C. 4th

Here are the answers to this block of questions...

A41. In January 2018, Liverpool completed their record transfer fee – a staggering £75 million for a defender.

A42. Dutch defender Virgil van Dijk arrived for Southampton on 1st January 2018 in the club's record transfer deal.

A43. After protracted negotiations Liverpool received £142 million from Barcelona in January 2018 for a Brazilian midfielder, with the fee eclipsing the £75 million received from the same club in July 2014 for Luis Suarez.

A44. Philippe Coutinho was the player who moved to Barcelona for a record fee of £142 million.

A45. The first Liverpool player to get capped by England was Frank Becton on the 29th March 1897.

A46. Steven Gerrard won a grand total of 114 caps for England. He appeared a total of 12 times in the World Cup Finals too (Japan 2006, South Africa 2010 and Brazil 2014).

A47. It's a tie! Michael Owen scored 26 goals for England and Ian Rush scored 26 goals for Wales.

A48. Jerome Sinclair was just 16 years and 6 days old when he made his debut against West Bromwich Albion in September 2012.

A49. Michael Owen was just 17 years and 143 days old when he scored, on his debut, against Wimbledon on 6th May 1997.

A50. Liverpool finished the 2017/18 season in 4th place.

I hope you're learning some new facts about the Reds. Here's the next set of questions.

51. Who is Liverpool's oldest ever goal scorer?
    A. Ned Doig
    B. George Hodgson
    C. Billy Liddell

52. Who is the club's longest serving manager of all time?
    A. Jack Nicklaus
    B. Arnold Palmer
    C. Tom Watson

53. Who is the club's longest serving post war manager?
    A. Rafael Benitez
    B. Bob Paisley
    C. Bill Shankly

54. What is the name of Liverpool's match day programme?
    A. Liverpool FC Match Day Programme
    B. Anfield Match Day Programme
    C. Merseyside Musings

55. Which of these is a Liverpool fanzine?
    A. Red All Over The Land
    B. The Scouse Way
    C. Mersey Beats

56. What animal is on the club crest?
    A. Crown Bird
    B. Liver Bird
    C. Billy Bird

57. How much did Gillett and Hicks pay for the club in 2006?
    A. £218.9 million

B.   £248.9 million
C.   £278.9 million

58. How much did Fenway Sports Group pay for the club in 2010?
A.   £300 million
B.   £400 million
C.   £500 million

59. What could be regarded as the club's most well known song?
A.   You Will Never Walk Alone
B.   Fearless
C.   The Fields of Athenry

60. Which ex-player was European Footballer of The Year in 1978 and 1979?
A.   Kevin Keegan
B.   Ian Rush
C.   Graeme Souness

Here are the answers to this block of questions.

A51. Billy Liddell was 38 years and 55 days old when he scored against Stoke City on the 5th March 1960.

A52. Tom Watson is the club's longest serving manager of all time. He held the position from 1896 until his death in 1915, a total of 19 years. During his tenure, the club won the League twice.

A53. The incomparable Bill Shankly is the club's longest serving post war manager. He was in charge of 783 games from December 1959 to July 1974.

A54. The catchy name of the match day programme is the Liverpool FC Match Day Programme.

A55. Red All Over the Land Fanzine is probably the best known of the Liverpool fanzines.

A56. A liver bird is on the club crest. It is based upon the city's coat of arms where the liver bird is prominent. The current crest dates from 1999.

A57. The club was valued at £218.9 million, including the club's debts, when Gillett and Hicks took over in 2006. They paid £174.1 million for the shareholding and £44.8 million to cover the club's debts.

A58. Fenway bought the club in October 2010 for £300 million.

A59. You Will Never Walk Alone is of course the club's most well known song.

A60. It was Super Kev - Kevin Keegan who won the European Footballer of The Year awards in 1978 and 1979. He received the prestigious awards whilst playing for German club Hamburg, having moved there in the summer of 1977.

Let's give you some easy questions.

61. What is the traditional colour of the home shirt?
    A. Red
    B. White
    C. Blue

62. What is the traditional colour of the away shirt?
    A. Green
    B. Purple
    C. White

63. Who introduced the all red kit?
    A. Joe Fagan
    B. Bob Paisley
    C. Bill Shankly

64. Who is the current club sponsor?
    A. HSBC
    B. Standard Chartered
    C. UBS

65. Who was the first club sponsor?
    A. Hitachi
    B. Carlsberg
    C. Crown Paints

66. Which of these have once sponsored the club?
    A. Candy
    B. Mandy
    C. Randy

67. Who is currently the club chairman?
    A. Martin Broughton
    B. George Gillett
    C. Tom Werner

68. Who was the club's first foreign signing, excluding South Africans?
    A. Xabi Alonso
    B. Avi Cohen
    C. Robert Rudram

69. Who was the club's first black player?
    A. John Barnes
    B. Howard Gayle
    C. Mark Walters

70. Who was the club's first match in the league against?
    A. Middlesbrough Ironopolis
    B. Newcastle Metropolis
    C. Sunderland Supertropolis

Here are the answers to the last set of questions.

A61. The answer is red. If you got that wrong, you should be ashamed of yourself!

A62. From 1921-1977 the colour of the away shirt was white. Since then it has been a right mixture, encompassing white, yellow, black, grey and green - in a right mix of shades, but historically the first choice away kit colour has to be white.

A63. In November 1964, Bill Shankly had a brainwave: to send the team out in all red. In doing away with white socks and trim, Shanks thought his team would be more intimidating. We all know the answer.

A64. Standard Chartered Bank is the current club sponsor. They are a British multi-national and financial services company employing over 80,000 people worldwide.

A65. Liverpool FC were the first professional English football club to finalise a shirt sponsorship deal and have a sponsor's logo emblazoned on their kit. 1979, the Reds agreed to a deal with Japanese electronic giants Hitachi and a famous Liverpool kit was born and history made. At that time the Liverpool kit was manufactured by Umbro, which continued until 1985.

A66. In 1988 Candy took over sponsorship of the club. Candy is an Italian owner manufacturer of household appliances, most famous of which are their washing machines. This Liverpool kit was the last one to see the Reds win a league title with, and for this reason will be forever part of Liverpool's history.

A67. American businessman Tom Werner is the current club chairman.

A68. Avi Cohen signed for Liverpool in July 1979, making his debut two months later, and he was the club's first foreign signing excluding the eight South Africans who had played for the club during the years 1903 to 1933.

A69. Toxteth born Howard Gayle was the club's first black player, making his debut in October 1980. He only made five appearances in total.

A70. Middlesbrough Ironopolis were Liverpool's first ever opponents in the Football League, in the Second Division on 2nd September 1893. Liverpool won 2-0.

I hope you are enjoying this book. Let's move on to the next block of questions.

71. How many goals did Ian Rush score for Liverpool during his career?
    A. 334
    B. 346
    C. 358

72. How many people died as a result of the Hillsborough disaster in 1989?
    A. 76
    B. 86
    C. 96

73. How many people died in the Heysel disaster in 1985?
    A. 19
    B. 29
    C. 39

74. Who is considered as Liverpool's main rivals?
    A. Everton
    B. Manchester United
    C. Tranmere Rovers

75. What shirt number did John Barnes wear?
    A. 8
    B. 10
    C. 11

76. What shirt number did Jamie Carragher wear?
    A. 13
    B. 23
    C. 33

77. Who was the oldest first-team player for the club?
    A. Phil Neal

B. Ned Doig
C. Elisha Scott

78. How old was he at the time?
    A. 40 years and 135 days
    B. 41 years and 165 days
    C. 42 years and 117 days

79. When did Liverpool win the European Cup for
    the first time?
    A. 1976
    B. 1977
    C. 1978

80. Who did they beat in the final?
    A. Bayer Leverkusen
    B. Bayern Munich
    C. Borussia Munchengladbach

Here are the answers to the last set of questions.

A71. Ian Rush scored 346 goals for the Reds, in his 660 appearances in two spells for the club.

A72. 96 people died as a result of The Hillsborough disaster. At the centre of the Hillsborough Memorial at Anfield is an eternal flame, signifying that those who died will never be forgotten.

A73. In the European Cup Final of 1985 at the Heysel stadium in Brussels, charging Liverpool supporters fans caused a wall to collapse leading to the death of 39 Juventus supporters. Fourteen Liverpool fans were found guilty of manslaughter. The disaster led to English clubs being banned from European competitions for five years.

A74. Everton or Manchester United are the club's main rivals. We will accept either answer.

A75. PFA Player of the Year for 1988 John Barnes, nicknamed Tarmac, aka the Black Heighway, wore the number 10 shirt.

A76. Jamie Carragher's shirt number was 23.

A77. Goalkeeper Ned Doig was the oldest player ever to play for the club.

A78. Ned was 41 years and 165 days when he played against Newcastle United in April 1908, making him the club's oldest ever player. It is a record that is unlikely to ever be broken. Liverpool told Doig his career was over by having a postcard delivered to his door which said "Your services are no longer required."

A79. Liverpool won the European Cup for the first time on the 25th May 1977.

A80. Liverpool beat Borrusia Monchengladbach 3-1 in the Olympic Stadium in Rome. The Liverpool goal scorers were Terry McDermott, Tommy Smith and Phil Neal. Of the starting eleven and five substitutes, one was Welsh, one was Irish and the other fourteen were English. How times have changed!

I hope you're learning some new facts about the club.
Here's the next block of ten questions.

81. Who was the first Liverpool player to feature in a
World Cup Finals tournament?
   A. Laurie Hughes
   B. Laurie Hunt
   C. Laurie Hunter

82. For which country did he feature at the World Cup?
   A. England
   B. Spain
   C. Germany

83. Who was Liverpool's first non-British player to
appear in a World Cup final?
   A. Pepe Reina
   B. Dietmar Hamann
   C. Fernando Torres

84. For which country did he play?
   A. Germany
   B. Spain
   C. Brazil

85. Who were the first non-British Liverpool World
Cup winners?
   A. Pepe Reina and Fernando Torres
   B. Luis Suarez and Enrique
   C. Ian Callaghan and Roger Hunt

86. Who are the current official kit suppliers to
Liverpool?
   A. Adidas
   B. New Balance
   C. Warrior Sports

87. What is the name of the official club website?
   A. liverpoolfc.com

B. koptalk.com
C. thisisanfield.com

88. Who among these players was the first World Cup winner?
    A. Dietmar Hamann
    B. Roger Hunt
    C. Fernando Torres

89. Who were the first Liverpool managers?
    A. Matt McQueen and Tom Watson
    B. John McKenna and W. E. Barclay
    C. Tom Watson and Tom Werner

90. Who is the longest-serving Liverpool manager by matches?
    A. Tom Watson
    B. Bill Shankly
    C. Bob Paisley

Here are the answers to this block of questions.

A81. Liverpool's first representative in a World Cup was Laurie Hughes, a scouser who had signed for the club in 1943.

A82. Laurie Hughes made three appearances for England in the World Cup tournament in Brazil in 1950, including the 1-0 defeat by USA.

A83. Dietmar Hamann was Liverpool's first non-British player to appear in a World Cup final.

A84. Dietmar Hamann represented Germany. He made 59 appearances for the national side, including starting in the final in Japan when Germany lost 2-0 to Brazil.

A85. Pepe Reina and Fernando Torres were the first non-British Liverpool World Cup winners. Reina and Torres represented Spain when they won the 2010 World Cup in South Africa, defeating Holland 1-0 in the final. Ian Callaghan and Roger Hunt both got winners medal back in 1966, but they were of course English.

A86. New Balance are the current Liverpool kit supplier, having taken over form Warrior Sports in time for the 2018/19 season.

A87. LiverpoolFC.com is the official club website, although there are a number of terrific unofficial websites.

A88. Roger Hunt was the first winner of a World Cup, appearing in England's 4-2 victory over Germany at Wembley in 1966. He played in all six of England's games in that successful campaign, scoring three times.

A89. John McKenna and W. E. Barclay were the first managers, being in charge from February 1892 to August 1896.

A90. Although the club's longest serving manager in time was Tom Watson who managed for 19 years from 1896 to 1915, the honour of the longest serving manager by matches goes to Bill Shankly. Shanks was in charge for 783 games, whilst Watson was in charge for 742 games.

Let's wind up with the final set of questions.

91. Who was the manager when Liverpool won the treble of League Cup, FA Cup and UEFA Cup in 2001?
   A. Rafael Benitez
   B. Kenny Dalglish
   C. Gerard Houlier

92. Which of these sports has taken part at Anfield?
   A. Boxing
   B. Rugby League
   C. Tennis

93. What postcode is Anfield in?
   A. L4
   B. L6
   C. L8

94. What is the highest European attendance ever recorded in the club's history?
   A. 55,104
   B. 55,446
   C. 58,757

95. Who was the opposition for the highest ever attendance in a European game?
   A. Bayern Munich
   B. Barcelona
   C. Borussia Dortmund

96. What is the lowest European attendance ever recorded in the club's history?
    A. 10,102
    B. 11,210
    C. 12,021

97. What is the record lowest attendance ever?
    A. 1,000
    B. 4,000
    C. 7,000

98. What shirt number does Jordan Henderson wear?
    A. 8
    B. 14
    C. 20

99. What does the sign above the stairs leading down to the pitch say?
    A. Come On You Reds
    B. This is Anfield
    C. You Will Never Walk Alone

100. What nickname did the fans give to Kenny Dalglish?
    A. The Flying Scotsman
    B. Genius Jock
    C. King Kenny

101. Outside the ground there is a statue of which former manager?
    A. Rafael Benitez
    B. Bob Paisley
    C. Bill Shankly

Here are the answers to the last set of questions.

A91. Gerard Houlier was in his second season as manager when Liverpool won the cup treble.

A92. It's a trick question as all have taken place! Boxing was often held at Anfield in the inter war years. Fred Perry and Bill Tilden played an exhibition tennis match in 1958. A Rugby League match was held between Australian side Penrith Panthers and Wigan Warriors in 1991 in front of over 20,000 spectators.

A93. Anfield is in the L4 postcode area.

A94. The highest ever attendance for a European match was 55,104.

A95. The highest ever attendance for a European match was against Barcelona in the 1975-76 season

A96. Just 12,021 spectators watched the European Cup first round, second leg tie against Dundalk in September 1982 during the 1982/83 season with Liverpool winning 1-0. Liverpool had won the first leg away 4-1.

A97. The lowest ever attendance is just 1,000, for a match against Loughborough in the 1895-96 season.

A98. Current club captain Jordan Henderson wears shirt number 14.

A99. The sign says "This is Anfield". Over the years there is no doubt it has served to intimidate the opposition.

A100. Kenneth Mathieson Dalglish MBE was nicknamed King Kenny. Incidentally he is Scotland's most capped player of all time, making 102 appearances for his country.

A101. Outside the Kop, there is a bronze statue of Bill Shankly. The statue plinth bears the inscription "He made the people happy".

That's a great question to finish with. That's it. I hope you enjoyed this ebook, and I hope you got most of the answers right. I also hope you learnt one or two new things about the club.

Printed in Poland
by Amazon Fulfillment
Poland Sp. z o.o., Wrocław